THOUGHTS, MEMORIES & DREAMS

ANSHIT BHARDWAJ

ISBN 979-888521889-4

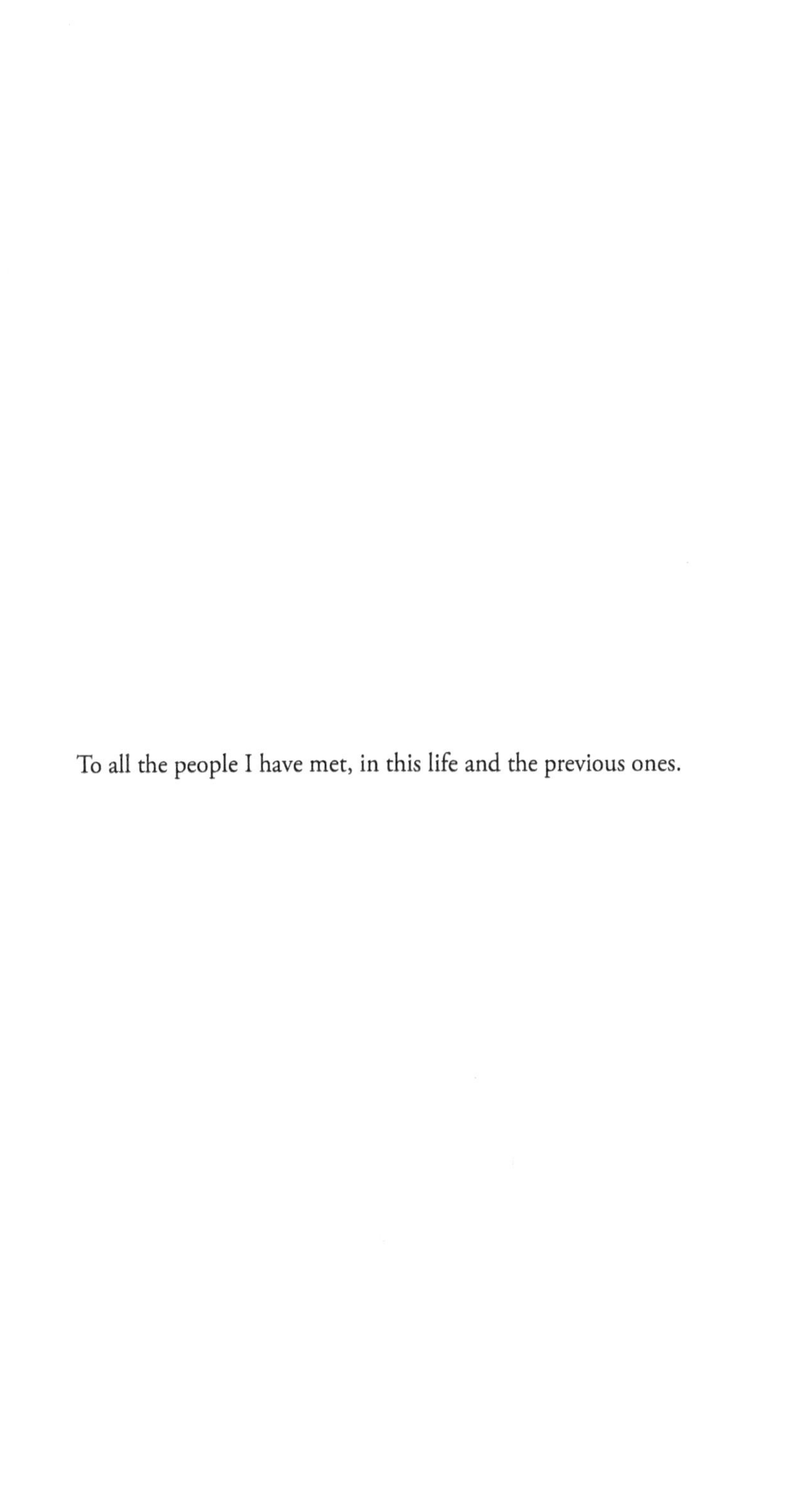

To all the people I have met, in this life and the previous ones.

Contents

Contents

Preface

Henry David Thoreau wrote that books must be read as deliberately as they were written. These poems have been written without any kind of deliberation.

Thoughts

1. 1

we see that folly is everywhere
in the daylight . the streams
flowing out of the mountains.
we carry ourselves around
like clouds floating endlessly,
waiting for rain
but folly is to find sunlight instead,
that's what we think.

2. 2

have i lost the desire to be free
how many days are being spent
in trying to undertake this arduous journey
with myself.
being alone has become a habit
one which is hard to quit.
the trance like state induced
from the stories manifests
in the funeral pyre of my passions.
is there a way to leave meaning behind
and keep sharing the events of my life,
narrating each little detail with reverence
to feel love for the things far away from my possessions;
as I watch people
from the window
that hangs over my office desk

3. 3

i have been searching continually
trying to improve the self,
and all the others that
come with it,
for free.
who can help
except these thoughts that take me,
drag me from one corner of my bed to the other.
is there a place where i can hide
and nobody will be able to see me,
or is there an open garden where i can ruin the best songs of all
time
and mind nobody's business.
but i know that i have come far,
before the dawn there was silence
i hope to carry it forward to the entire day
as time passes through me
and memories become my only bank account.
but as soon as i'm done with my morning prayer
and go out in the sun
"how are you", they'll ask
even if i'm not, i will say "fine"

i will listen to them patiently
till their opinion becomes mine.

• 6 •

4. 4

look at how far i've come
each night hopes for sun
miles away destiny lies
in no time, time flies
who is with me
who will cry
who tells the truth
who pretends to lie
how can two fingers
bear the weight of a hand
how can i sleep
and at the same time stand
where glory is, only peace was promised
to wake up one another
our minds were accustomed
but can anybody see me as a kid
treat me like my mother did
twice that stupid i want to be
your ideals cannot set me free
where is that land of joy
where is trouble, all but noise
neither a pilgrim, nor a saint

trying to breathe as i wait
i'm tired of getting lost in this paradigm
now i'm tired of wasting time
never to be bothered i want to stay
never to be found, never to crave.
far on the hill, he resides
i will try to pack my bags
before he tries
as the mist won't go out by itself
yet the seeds will sprout when it's wet
forgetting my name is virtue of the self
as far as the eye sees, there are only cries for help
but i do believe that somewhere skies are burned
somewhere, our prayers are heard
so allow yourself to hold your hand
decisions are spontaneous, accidents are planned

5. 5

as we move forward
we must watch each other's steps
for we know each one of us is afraid
and many things in out hearts are kept,
safe to be brought out only when
we become storytellers
recounting the nightmare we had last night
or poets,
reciting the confusion we feel inside.
but it is only in these moments
that we can figure out whether we are blessed
in the fire of chaos, all friendships are put to test.
everything burns
and the smoke emerging is addictive
once you taste it, it makes you selective
of what to wear on your sleeve, how many times to watch the
clock,
and when to do nothing;
water kindly washes away the arrogant rock.
so seek that
for which you were given birth
allow leaves to float in your swimming pool

THOUGHTS, MEMORIES & DREAMS

and be a human of worth.

6. 6

parallel dimensions
call you forth
lose your name
and find your worth.
lie down
when you wish to rise,
nod your head to reject
it's so foolish to be wise.
how many vanities
you keep safe in your bank
the sailor jumped out of the ship
before it sank.
twenty four hours are given to you to rest,
yet you turn each moment into a test.

7.7

and you give me advice
what is the point of life
i have roamed in the bazaars
crying out, trying to laugh
but time forgets my pains
as happiness dissolves in the fleeting sound of rain
two footprints matched my thoughts
i thought i had given it all
but i was wrong
yesterday was better than now
remembering who i am, but how?
what will be lost if i don't carry on,
except a life i don't deserve
heartbreaks have been giving me hope,
my only source of entertainment.
i say i love to live
but then why am i afraid of death
aren't light and shadow
incomplete without each other?
hoping is too much to bear
around a pagan who wants to disappear
to be whole again the battle is to be fought

in the corners of my mind, my dreams rot
how can i make a decision
when i have abandoned the gift of thought
revering the air,
the water gets hot.

8. 8

god above!
there's panic on the road
everytime things fall apart
look down at your home.
partition has been done
to the ones who made us sin
justice shall be served
at the hour of dawn,
when the sunlight begins
to suffice the sky blue
then i shall rise
to be honest with you.
see we haven't talked a lot
your edifice i kept erect in my heart
the spontaneity was lost
when time obscured our past.
be like the grass
that careens over water
swiftly it prophesises
the sonorous day of future.
hello to you my friend
who knows except you

that there is but hope
for them who cry at night.
if i cease to travel i will be carried to that land
where all possessions are rust,
where all glories are bland.
maybe then i can see
how rare it is to look
how effortlessly we search for our stories,
in someone else's book.
the one who discerns facts is an existentialist,
a puritan refuses to think
whatever endears along the way
leads the scholastic ship to sink.

9.9

tenderness is blessed
when outrageous thoughts
are bestowed on your future.
it's okay to be afraid,
nothing wrong with shedding tears
but sane is the man
who lets go of the mountain,
in order to see the world from above.
as time floats in your mind
you can't keep telling yourself
that one day you'll make it
or its all going to be fine.
wisdom cannot be purchased by trading words.
not even in your thoughts
to be old when you're young
and passionate on your deathbed,
there is something
something that must be sought
without actually seeking it
something that one is to attain
just to give it away
to himself

once again

10. 10

for the days behind the scenes
there are moments to be felicitated
again on the brink of salvation
tumbling of youth is dissipated.
how secure can a man be
before the snowflakes melt
reward won't be passionate,
seducing oneself is the test.
there were nights and mornings
then there was a blanket of pain
we slept in that blanket
now are the nights or mornings to blame?
he tried to be two persons
rains coveted the fragile sand
planning to come up with solutions,
he's only got two hands.
sometimes the sky covers,
sometimes it reflects
we all are mortgaged by opinions
when will you pay back the debt?

11. 11

like the stars above it's all going down
i thought i was king, but turned out to be a clown.
everyday with each thought
i keep track of the breaths i've got.
need to rest and keep my mind awake
got to sleep early so i can wake up late.
reality is a such porn
i always chase what i'm running from.
my arms are ready, my hands are heavy
the present is past already.
you will make all my lies come true
when i come to visit you.
i will have dinner
and then break the dishes,
i will step on your heart
while reaching for riches.
when you visit my home i will be out of town
like the stars above, everything is going down.

12. 12

it happens apparantly
that a thought crosses the mind
and i'm able to catch it
before i get left behind
to ask the questions
that have no answers
like a river, it flows
it's destination, it does not know.
but who's the thinker behind these thoughts
whose mind is it after all?
winter came and spring went,
now summer begins
on the banks of the holy river,
the thinker ceases to think.

Memories

13. 13

i finally found you
while stumbling upon broken promises
i finally let you see the truth
while you made me hold my breath.
so this time it begins
no friends, only us
leaving paradise, taking nothing.
even though i lost everything
thoughts are so clear,
i don't even want to think anymore.
i think i can feel the breeze,
the sun setting and water splashing.
real life has just begun.
i'm addicted to your eyes
so give me all your sufferings
let's live off an island
maybe i'm dreaming, maybe it's true
but i don't want your memories to disappear.
real meaning is found only in your words
thoughts are so clear i think i know what you mean
whenever you look away, whenever you clench your fists
i know myself much more than before

so much i've dived in your soul

14. 14

i ran into the thinnest aisles
to find your ghost breathing
to swoon over the time that had descended over us,
to evoke those revealations i had had when i was a child.
like an oracle, you wrote the fate of my visceral responses
you elicited warmth from my heart and made my mind burn in
the fire of hedonism
you had transcended my thoughts into a curb of posthumous
austerity.
time always ran ahead of us though
we tried to follow him
but he leaves no footsteps behind.
when the morning had dawned its miracles upon us
we sat by the lake, fawning over the days wasted without having
our hands hold each other.
and the day we parted, your scent filled my cosmic chasm with
eternal grace
my metaphysical possesions intruded your solace
our awareness put us in an oblivious daze.
we sat by the lake again
and thought about each other.

15. 15

i had been embracing slumber for eternity
pale and sterile, the days would pass
and i'd be busy painting the canvas of the sky
with my cloud like thoughts.
it was a warm breath of air that gently caressed my eyelashes
and soft fingertips calmly tipped over my palm,
some scent kissed my nostrils and
i came upon breaking my oblivion.
the windows were open now, the mirror had been wiped, the
floor was cleaned
it was the brightest moonlight when I woke up.
next day descended like a warm blanket over my body.
i was busy making castles of sand
when i realised i had been carried along with the tide,
i slept on the sand only to be woken up by raindrops drenching
my body.
you came to me when my eyelids began to wander, but lips still
chapped,
i saw you searching for your reflection in my mirror
i wished to call your name and build more castles with you
time suddenly stopped when i realised the rain i had always
danced in,

were fresh teardrops of your eyes.

16. 16

the night is drawing
the morning is calling.
at the same time
my heart skips a beat
when you look at the moon
don't forget my tears
that flow for you,
for you only.
and when i've done it all
when i've been what i always wanted to be
i couldn't look myself in the eye,
as you threw stones on my window.
so when you walk my path,
when the wind crawls
and the sunflowers bloom
i will be waiting
for eternity, for eternity
to try to love myself
for when the night dawns
and the morning calls
i don't forget
how much you love me.

17. 17

sitting among the ever changing senses
i perceive the world with nothing more than
some memories
memories that lay unguarded in my casket like brain,
even after their death they spring up
and contaminate the temple of my heart.
now, am i moving around the world pushed by these desires
or is it the world that keeps on revolving on the axis of my soul?
alone again, left to be mistreated
by the treachery of my feeling, i watched the clouds floating
above.
giving me hope at times to see the beauty in little things
and the mountains calling me to be their guest.
but when the night arrives, the thoughts during the day are
dissolved into darkness
and again,
i was crying while laughing
seeing the times change like my thoughts
i fled into venerable literature
to seek liberation from shackles that bind myself from running
with my mind.
seeking love inside a heart of gold,

i found a vast emptiness
encouraging me to go forth
while reclining to my soul simultaneously

18. 18

time has washed the memories of my childhood days
working hard to kindle faith in myself
i remember things yet to do.
no longer shall i be misled by intuition
to be alone,
i need to achieve something new.
blindfolded by my passions
does make sleeping a chore,
looking for beauty
then i saw a mountain
aren't you moving anymore,
silently cried the gypsy.
in return i raised my head, smiled and said
does anyone remember laughter?
last night rushing through a self help book
i stumbled upon some words and fell into a phrase that
resounded my state of mind
why should i travel when my limbs feel extended everywhere
everything mine, everything all too divine.
devoutly i bow my head before the mirror
what are the mountains saying to me
build a life instead of a career

being able to breathe is suffice,
what else probably could be the purpose of your life?
in return with tears in my eyes i bowed head and asked
where is sorrow now?
i saw a mountain
aren't you moving anymore
silently cried the gypsy
being able to breathe is suffice
what else, probably
could be the purpose of your life?

19. 19

used to be alone, but now i'm on my own
again to be misfired at the tender overture
another moment shall be a destiny's lifetime
to be yours i need to see through our desires
to be happy seems a avarcious duty now
apart from trying to be myself
i lean towards the excellence of numerology.
i stepped back and forth and realised what my true name was
for a life of glory and pride,
i slaughtered my once beloved childhood.
you met me at an obnoxious time indeed
your soul wasn't ready to mate with mine
although i was alone and trying to be myself
atleast i had the courage to be silent
but then, your love was too conspicuous for my solitary
indignation
our dreams dropped over the catastrophe to malice
so nigh was your solace,
when the truant auspiciousness cloyingly concerned our bland
restraint,
apropos of the skullduggery of that corrosive trimuvirate
made our love docile and utterly insipid.

such grandeur!

20. 20

when i saw the rain
i felt like i was drowning.
over here everything is wet
and the mist isn't compassionate enough
to allow one to see
another fellow running for shelter.
the orchards get lonely
it gets as cold as winter
the cattles sleep and my nose freezes.
it's only when oh!
the sun burns the overcast
and mellow sunlight gradually begins to bring soothing warmth
do people pray for rain here

21. 21

was it even worth it
to be able to breathe again?
found exasperation in my soul,
rooting for nothing but pain.
after such monotonous sincerity
being obidient is like a chore
you have forgotten to open your hands,
yet you keep asking for more.
about an obnoxious day
was that with which our shadows split
few moments are tacit as your words
nothing is as tactile as your wit.
i was a connoisseur
who mistook myself as an art
it's like running a treadmill now,
perplexed where to start.
another reason to stay alive
is to be a remedy when you're mad
as a part of myself,
i secretly stuffed inside your bag.
everything is orthodox
when they don't give a fuck

you have it in abundance,
could i borrow some luck?

22. 22

the night eludes my dreams,
where have you been?
obsessed with me i call out your name
trying to ask you out , take your hand in mine
trying to call you mine.
is it that good to listen songs together
and trying to write one for ourselves
this is something i never knew,
something i always wanted.
how many people we met randomly
asking what were they to become
and hanging out in the parks
where you kissed me in front of everyone
whatever you think i know and when i feel nothing
you make me fall asleep.
and that's what i want baby,
fingers running through your hair
while i try to write songs.
let's party tonight
let's find out what we have become
you wearing your favourite dress
and i promise tomorrow will never come.

they like to drink and dance
we can't be happier when we just want to have fun
no need to figure anything out
as you talk to me
i'll put words in your mouth.
i like to drive your car
and go over and over,
but to the same time
when you saw me as a flower.
you took everything from me
but you didn't give a fuck
i was looking at you
but you didn't pick me up.
and that's why i love you too
leave me behind so i can follow you.
all the time knowing
that actually you pray whenever you move.
can't everyone see
you hate my songs
to bring out the poetry in me.

23. 23

wish i could talk some more
wish i could make up those excuses again
you've left behind so many memories
wish you and i could be the same.
how sure were you
didn't even think twice
when i couldn't trust myself
you used to believe my lies.
i remember how you held my hand
the sunshine and the clouds,
whenever i didn't want to go home
you made me laugh it out.
can still recall your smile
each thing you taught me
how did those days pass
i had no company.
only your advices to console
and your mischiefs to make me laugh
in the orchards i want to lie down,
in the stormy nights i want to dance.
no matter what was said
the weather always told me the truth

they had me,
i had you.
there was not a day
when you didn't make me smile
ah! the blessed fruits
we used to keep away.
refuge i took in your arms
maybe that's what gave me the strength
twice as young i was,
the sweetness of your eyes and the warmth of your palms
even your robust mood swings
were but an act to stop me from crying
beautiful mornings they used to be
with the birds you used to sing,
and there's not a thing i didn't let you know
i only used to feel, didn't bother to think.
wish i could tell you my secrets again
wish you could chase me till I can't catch my breath.
want to speak my mind to you
want to look out of the window with you while it rains.
love is forever and it is true
that we don't talk too much,
but while others look for happiness
i raise my eyelids to you.
and you, all the gifts you brought
i should've kept safe in my locker
i was self taught,

excuse me for my behavior.
following you always
to throw away your books
must've been a chore
missing all the things i took.
without your permission
but somehow i knew you didn't mind
your angry face could never hide your smile.
so was our little playground
you and me always together
be it the grasslands or the trees
i always knew you were better.
at telling lies than me
i should pay back your debt
for all my shortcomings you've kept safely
scolding for dinner we would get.
had we been all day in each other's company
in my books i would search for new ways to tease you,
when you used to leave me behind
and each second spent to wait
how did it come to be,
that i grew up so quick
they ask me
i ask you.

24. 24

nights maybe of solace
if your hands are made of gold
you can only buy back,
what you once sold.
every heartbeat is a mystery
each footstep is a nod
all breaths whisper his name,
all roads lead to god.
when you were with me,
i left everything behind
forgot to lose you,
while i was chasing time.
never has there been a voice
that's louder than the word,
if you open the cage
you can capture the bird.
moments are lost
like leaves falling off a tree
listen before you speak
close your eyes before you see.
now the stream is back,
meandering in my heart

eternity slips away
when lovers like us part.

Dreams

25. 25

what does it mean to be alone?
is it the sprouting of spiritual seeds
amidst the bogus muck of the mind,
or is it to find a place where one can
indelibly be independent, and yet depend on nature

26. 26

when everything is fine,
do i ever look above
like a star that's falling i wait for my death at night
and when death arrives i smile at it,
and call it a day.
few things seem relevant to the anxieties i've overcome,
to the battles that were never won.
there's but fortune for those who cry
strangling their souls is their idea of getting high.
ofcourse the day is short
and breaths matter more than moments
but have i ever looked behind
to all the non sense that i've carried along to paradise?
never before i hated my fate so much
never before had my mind been in such haste
to cover up everything,
each inch of my guilt laid skin.
and this doesn't come out of stillness
i declare it to be a result of pure unconsciousness.
however, i have realised
that none of my thoughts are real
for they were imposed upon me

when i was busy daydreaming.
each mountain seems like a home now
did i ever look beside me,
how many things did i overlook
maybe this, maybe that
everything evaporates eventually,
all the candles burn down.
seeking happiness all the time
is this the cause of all misery
it feels like each moment is provoking me
to set out to be a pilgrim
and prove my worth as a human.
apparently, i was born to die one day
why not just be sure about it.

27. 27

a joy of touching the divine,
the nights waiting for the day,
leaps of faith towards god,
mistrust of my soul wandering love.
the day i became free i realised
to breathe can be old fashioned
without a sharp indignation.
to mock myself in sleep can be perilous
when i strike my chest,
the ephemeral guidance i decipher from the heavens.
some longing still prevails in my austere unambiguity
which is holding me upfront, constraint with my delusional self.
and with a flinch of introspection,
i auspiciously uncover the audacious fluttering off the page
i seek refuge under coveted words
which further elevate my lust for an ungraspable yet witheld
scarcity of knowledge.

28. 28

when i eat, it happens.
when i sit, it happens.
when i drink, it happens.
when i walk, it happens.
when i see, it happens.
when i speak, it happens.
when i dance, it happens.
when i write, it happens.
when i laugh, it happens.
when i kiss, it happens.
when i wonder, it happens.
when i breathe, it happens.
when i laugh, it happens.
it happens whenever i allow it to happen.

29. 29

how many years have passed
how many days did i miss
for my own well being i might be too self conscious,
but happiness is contagious in a world around people like you.
i have been trying to get over my solitary indignation
to reduce my thoughts to wicks of devotion
passing time feels like water washing my dirty feet
and the sun being too conspicious to let me shine in front of him.
at the same time i ask myself what have i become after all this
mess
love might be dying, hope is getting on it's knees
have i totally forgotten to conclude
what had i initiated?
the master seeks the seeker
as much as my inability to express myself
in psychoanalysis, this thing is cool.
even after getting all good times slaughtered
some desires still linger around, like ghosts.
and one of them is to be reborn,
again.

30. 30

how does a leaf bear the winter winds
i wonder when they tell me i'm worthless
only when there is no life in their hearts
do people care about making a living.
here everything is destined
even the number of breaths are counted
keeping record of each sigh, each sneeze
has made me wonder if i'm any better than i used to be.
am i doing justice to the role i'm destined to play?
infinite are the lessons
and precise the moments
which make men doubt themselves
after which every friendly advice is a toxic relationship
and no matter what lies in the year to come
only those who can chop wood
are the ones who will survive snowfall.

31. 31

i have wished for peace
dreamt of fleeting time,
with no intention to sit.
how many roads diverge,
whereupon a poet gives an ear
to the transient noises of nature.
i have in my sorrows
tried to be that artist
who can listen while getting bored.
there were clouds, so it couldn't rain
no use of tracking each day's progress.
i have often asked myself
if there is another me
who dreams of all this as well.
but only the open air upon the silent meadows.
after all,
who ever could stay silent while his house was on fire?
only an artist who thinks he has failed.

32. 32

hey!

it's me.

i've been a dormant formality

twice as concerned as you,

but always under your blanket.

your solace cannot be confounded

your jeopardy is slithering,

against a reprimanding turmoil

your sovereignty has exuded.

somber stem solicited the hay,

the opulence of the discarded stone.

however, some wildlife has to be presented

at the patriarchal commemoration.

let the night be still

allow me to take some pleasure

seeing your face is a solistice

let's row south for treasure.

to take care of yourself you must let me in

drown my tears in your skin.

so, before the verdict is laid

before the flight takes off,

give me your number

and pick up my call.

33. 33

sometimes moments are empty handed
carrying the gift of miracles
they blend an inescapable dichotomy
for the ones who don't value them.
now, being alone is alright
but at what cost?
are you willing to trade
your memories for pleasures
your pleasures for pains.
i agree that you must take time
to try to be yourself
but i'd rather be guilty of incompetence,
than taking my own life.

34. 34

moving ahead beyond time
so many wasted moments.
in trying to believe in oneself,
so many unnecessary laments.
before there was time
how were the days?
after death,
that will remain.
a little bit friendly
was talking about sadness.
everyone feels the same
when they're treated as guests.
so the sage is busy,
while being distracted.
yet reducing himself,
the play is acted.

35. 35

revere the end of knowledge
each day is a triumph
war is waged on the already defeated
to provide for each miserable reprisal.
deferred were my emotions,
neither the stick nor the stone
hold the air in my hand
can it be a storm?
however beautiful you are
it's all in my head.
there i break walls
there i go to rest.
if i could aimlessly roam
i would ask you to come along.